THE HAUNTED STARSHIP

By Joy Cowley

Illustrated by E. Silas Smith

DOMINIE PRESS
Pearson Learning Group

Paperback ISBN 0-7685-1092-9
Printed in Singapore
   5 6 7 8   09

Dominie
Press
Pearson Learning Group

1-800-321-3106
www.pearsonlearning.com

Table of Contents

Chapter One
The Wreck

From their new apartment on the 260th floor, Conrad could see the wrecked starship. His bedroom window was near the clear wall of the dome that covered the city. On the other side of the dome was a huge Martian dust lake, and by the edge of the red lake there was a tiny, silver glint.

When Conrad looked at the glint through his mother's laser glasses, he saw that it was an old passenger shuttle with its nose buried in red dust.

"Did you come from Earth on one of those?" he asked his mother.

She shook her head. "They were long before

my time, Conrad. Two hundred years ago, there was a big fleet of those shuttles going between Mars and Earth. You can still see them in Astro Museums."

Conrad studied the ship through the glasses. It didn't look all that old. "Why didn't they put this one in a museum?"

"It's used for storage."

"Storage?" He moved the glasses and saw a high wire fence around the wreck. "You mean—treasure?"

She shook her head. "No. Toxic waste. Toxic material that's too dangerous to be dumped. That's why no one's allowed to go there."

Conrad lowered the glasses. "You know what I heard at school?"

"What did you hear?" She took the laser glasses from him and put them back in their case.

"The real reason no one goes there is because it's haunted." He looked toward the wreck, a speck of silver near the horizon. "It's full of ghosts from the people who died in the crash."

"Oh, Conrad! Where do you get these silly stories?"

"The other kids told me," he said. "They say you can hear screaming voices. The skeletons get up and walk around."

His mother laughed and laughed. "Jumping jets! What next?"

"They say it's true!" he cried.

She put her hand to her mouth as though she were trying to stop the laughter from coming out. "Conrad, honey, people did die in that crash, but their bodies weren't left on board. There are no skeletons. There are no ghosts."

"But the kids at school..."

She put her arm around him. "Sometimes parents tell children scary stories to keep them away from dangerous places. But this is the truth. For years, the old wreck was a dumping ground for toxic waste—radioactive material, warfare chemicals. Things like that. That's all."

Conrad felt both relieved and disappointed. Something in him wanted to believe that the wreck was haunted.

His mother said, "Honey, we've come halfway around the planet to a new city. You're going to a new school, meeting new people, hearing new stories."

He shrugged, feeling the heaviness of her arm across his shoulders.

"It will take a while to sort out fact from fiction," she said. "But I'll tell you this, Conrad. I've commanded death ships. That's what they call ships with a tragic past. People have died on them. But I have never, ever seen a ghost."

"That's because you don't believe in ghosts," he said.

"Exactly," she said. "Ghosts only exist in your mind."

Chapter Two
Haunted?

Gamma was a brand new Martian city, and already Conrad liked it. They had moved from the old Alpha colony because his mother got a job with a freight firm in Gamma. She was the captain of the galactic ore carrier, *The Phoebus*. On the long trips, Conrad went with her. But if she was doing a short run, Conrad stayed with Plata and her parents, Mr. and Mrs. Arjee.

Plata, who was in Conrad's class at school, lived on the 89th floor. Her apartment didn't have a view, but it was a lot bigger than Conrad's, and it had an anti-gravity games room. Conrad and Plata played anti-gravity soccer, mid-air. It was a lot harder than the old gravity soccer. You kicked the ball with both feet, but there was no telling which way it would go.

Plata's parents were engineers, working for the same freight company as Conrad's mother. They were also new to Gamma. Mrs. Arjee designed cooling systems for new freight ships. Mr. Arjee was an eco-engineer. His job was pollution control. He had to make sure that the freight ships and their cargoes didn't cause damage to the Martian environment.

Conrad knew that Mr. Arjee went out of the dome every month to take soil samples for testing. He would be the best person to ask about the wrecked starship.

"I've been past it a couple of times," Mr. Arjee said. "No one can get too close. There are fences and *Keep Out* signs everywhere. It sure makes a joke of my job."

Conrad didn't understand. "A joke?"

"That old starship's full of toxic waste," he said.

Plata looked at Conrad. She tossed her curly black hair and said, "No, it's haunted."

"I wish it were," snorted Mr. Arjee. "Ghosts are make-believe. Pollution is real. We've got a wreck full of toxic waste right on our doorstep. No one wants to do anything about it. You'd think humans would have learned a lesson from what they did to Earth."

Plata was ready to argue with her father. "I think there are ghosts."

Conrad said, "Plata, Mom told me it was a dumping place."

"She was right," said Mr. Arjee. "It's full of

dangerous waste. It shouldn't be there. They should take it to some barren satellite."

But Plata wasn't ready to give up. She said, "There's this boy at school. His uncle went out to the starship, and he heard it. Things inside were screaming. Poisonous garbage doesn't scream."

Mr. Arjee smiled. "His space suit must have big ears."

But Plata wasn't amused. Conrad knew that she, too, wanted to believe the ghost story.

Chapter Three

Out of the Dome

The space suits were ultra-stress quality and very heavy. It was a struggle to get them on.

"I can't move in it!" Plata complained.

"Sorry," said Mr. Arjee, who didn't sound sorry at all. "If you're coming out with me, that's what you're wearing."

"But Dad, your suit's light," Plata whined.

"I have to walk around getting rock samples," her father said. "You two will be sitting in the jet cart. Now, do you want to go or don't you?"

Plata nodded.

"Then put your helmet on," said Mr. Arjee. "I'll check you both in a minute."

Conrad didn't complain. He'd lived in Gamma nearly six months and hadn't been out of the dome. There had been flights over Mars with his mother, but sitting in a freight wagon didn't count. It wasn't like bumping along the ground in a jet cart or stomping boot marks into red dust.

He thought the ultra-stress space suits were ridiculous, but he and Plata were both a little afraid of what they might find out at the starship wreck. Besides, Mr. Arjee wasn't taking any risks. When Conrad's mother came back, Mr. Arjee would tell her, "I took the children, but I made them wear ultra-stress suits." That would impress Conrad's mother. She would think that Mr. Arjee was very responsible.

Once their helmets were on, they had to use wrist controls to talk. The receivers in their helmets were new, and Plata's voice came through clearly. "I asked Dad to stop at the wreck."

Conrad pressed the communication button on his wrist. "What did he say?"

Plata grinned from behind her visor. "He said, *yes!*"

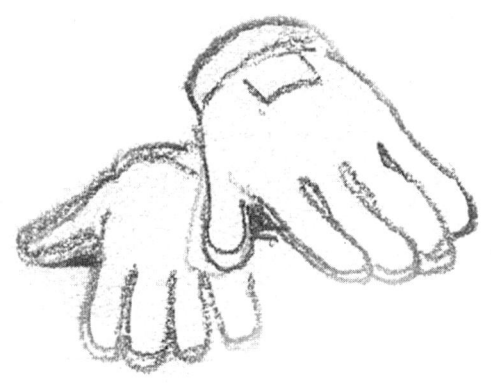

Chapter Four
Death Ship

Mr. Arjee checked their seat harnesses, then pulled down the jet cart's cover. The machine lifted gently from the platform outside the Arjees' door, and floated down the building.

Mr. Arjee was being careful. The cart drifted between tall apartments and finally came to rest at the main port. Mr. Arjee showed the guard their passes. They went through the port, through the inner hatch, and into the air lock. Moments later they were out in the hard, bright light of the Martian day. The jet cart was skimming over the red ground, with the cover down.

Conrad wondered what Mars would feel like without a space suit. People once lived without survival suits on planet Earth. That's what his mother said. In the old days on Earth, people didn't need domes. They could breathe the atmosphere and run around without wearing survival suits. Conrad shivered. If he took off his helmet he would last about two minutes.

The jet cart zipped fast over the dust lake. They were several feet above the lake, with the exhaust stream kicking up red clouds behind them that hid the city of Gamma. Ahead, the starship was getting closer. But they were still too far away to see the fence around it.

"Those were great old ships," said Mr. Arjee. "Anti-static exterior. Notice how the dust never sticks to it? Strong, too. It didn't break up when it came down."

Conrad pressed the button on his wrist. "What made it crash?" he asked.

Mr. Arjee said, "History tells us it was a crash landing. They lost their oxygen. The captain switched on the autopilot, and the shuttle came down by itself. But by that time all 360 passengers and crew were dead."

"Didn't they have survival suits?" Plata asked.

"Maybe there were a few suits on board," Mr. Arjee replied. "It wouldn't have made much difference."

They could now see the high steel fence and the broad stretch of the starship's fins.

"Wow! It's big!" Conrad cried.

"Oh yes, it's big all right," said Mr. Arjee. "Bigger even than your mom's ore carrier."

"Mom says when people have died on a ship it's called a 'death ship.' "

Mr. Arjee's voice came back into his helmet. "This shuttle will always be a death ship while it's full of toxic waste."

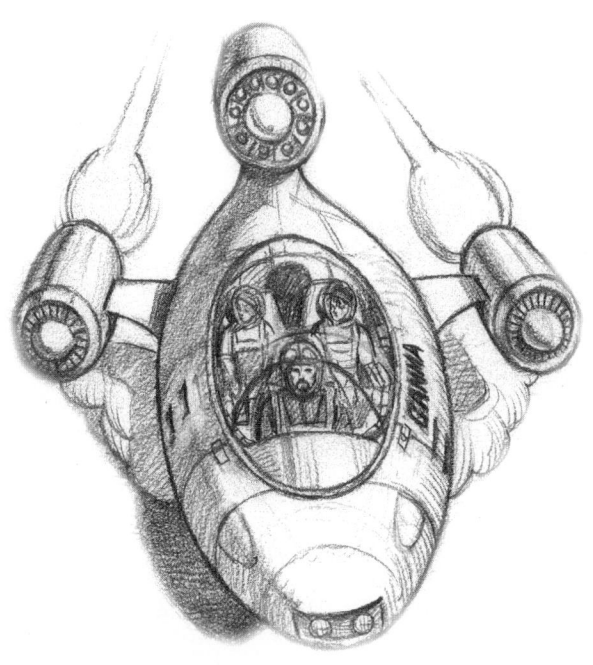

Chapter Five

At the Fence

Mr. Arjee took the jet cart twice around the old shuttle. "Seen enough?" he said.

"I want to get out," said Plata. "I want to walk around it."

"We have to move on," said Mr. Arjee. "I've got to collect rock samples."

"You can leave us here while you pick up the rocks," said Plata.

Mr. Arjee turned in his seat. "I'll do nothing of the kind."

"We'll be all right," said Plata. "What can happen to us?"

Mr. Arjee looked at Conrad. "You want to get out, too?"

Conrad squirmed inside his suit. "Yeah - if - if that's okay."

"Nothing can happen to us!" Plata insisted.

Plata was right. They were wearing suits that could go through fire or acid. They had eight hours of oxygen. If they weren't all back in the dome in two hours, the rescue guards would come out to find them.

Mr. Arjee brought the jet cart down onto red sand. "All right," he said. "I'll leave you here while I get the samples. But I'll be almost half an hour. You'll get bored."

"No, we won't," said Plata, undoing her harness.

"If there's any problem, call me and I'll be right back," said Mr. Arjee. He helped them out of the jet cart, first Plata and then Conrad. "I want you to promise me you won't touch that fence."

Conrad looked at the steel fence that towered above them. The mesh was thick and covered with sharp spikes. "I promise," he said.

Chapter Six

Caretaker

As the jet cart sped away, Conrad wondered if they'd done the right thing. Almost on the horizon was the small bubble of Gamma. Beside them was the starship wreck and the threatening fence with its *Keep Out* signs. Everything else was empty red desert.

"Listen!" said Plata. "Hear that?"

He listened and heard only the sound of his breathing.

"Turn up the volume on your helmet!" she cried.

He put his thickly gloved hands to his earpieces and felt for the volume controls. As he turned the knobs, he heard a high-pitched noise, more of a shriek than a scream. It was coming from the ship.

"Ghosts!" said Plata, her eyes bright behind her face plate.

Conrad unhooked a locator device from his belt and waved it toward the ship. A red light turned green when the arrows pointed toward the front of the shuttle. "I think it's coming from the control room," he said.

"It's haunted!" Plata yelled. "I knew it!" She tried to walk closer to the source of the noise. Conrad followed. The suits were so heavy, it was like carrying a desk. Four or five steps and they'd have to stop to gather more strength.

The shrieking noise was getting closer, louder. Then Plata stopped. Her right glove jabbed at her left wrist. "There's a door opening!" she yelled to Conrad.

She was right. On the side of the ship, not far from the buried nose cone, there was a dark gap. As they watched, it grew wider and a ramp began to slide toward the ground.

"It's the ghost!" Plata's voice was a squeak.

The figure that came out was anything but ghost-like. They saw someone in a tall blue-and-white space suit in the doorway, and a deep voice called, "You there! What are you doing?" Then the figure came down the ramp and toward them.

Conrad would have run if he had been able to. Then he thought, "This is silly! We've done nothing wrong."

"It's a guard," said Plata, taking a clumsy step backward.

"He's not wearing a guard's suit," said Conrad.

The man stopped on the other side of the

fence. Through the steel mesh they saw into his face plate, and then they relaxed. He had dark skin, warm brown eyes, and a friendly smile. His deep voice sounded in their ear pieces. "It must have been you two who set off my alarm."

"So that *was* an alarm we heard," Conrad said.

Plata looked up at the man's face plate. "Are you one of the guards?"

"I'm Jethro Anderson, the caretaker here," he replied. "It's my job to keep you safe. You'll have to move back. You're too close."

"We haven't touched the fence," Conrad said.

"You're still too close," said the caretaker. "This ship's been used as a dumping ground for toxic waste. Now some of it has become unstable. You shouldn't even be in the area."

Plata stood firm. She said, "I'm Plata Arjee,

and this is my friend Conrad. My father is the chief eco-engineer..."

"I know who you are," said the caretaker, "and your father wouldn't have left you here if he'd known what was in there. In a couple of days he'll do an air pollution test here. The high toxic levels will be discovered, and this site will be declared a disaster zone. The waste will be shipped to a safe dumping ground, light years from Mars." He waved his hand. "Don't stop. Keep walking."

They took another step backward, and another. "We're okay, Mr. Anderson," said Conrad. "We've got safety suits, high-density, ultra-stress..."

The caretaker didn't seem interested in their suits. He kept waving them back. They turned and plodded slowly: one step, then another step away from the fence. When they looked back, he was still there, waving at them. His voice, crackling with static, filled their ears. "That's not far enough. Keep going..."

Chapter Seven

Ghosts?

The jet cart settled beside them, and the cover flipped back. Mr. Arjee got out to help Conrad and Plata into their seats. "What are you doing way out here?" he said. "Ghosts scare you off?"

"Ha ha ha," said Plata. Her legs ached, and she was in a grumpy mood. "Very funny," she said.

Conrad was grateful for the assistance. He flopped into the back seat and let Mr. Arjee fix his seat harness.

"It was the caretaker," Conrad said. "He made us go miles away from the fence." He felt

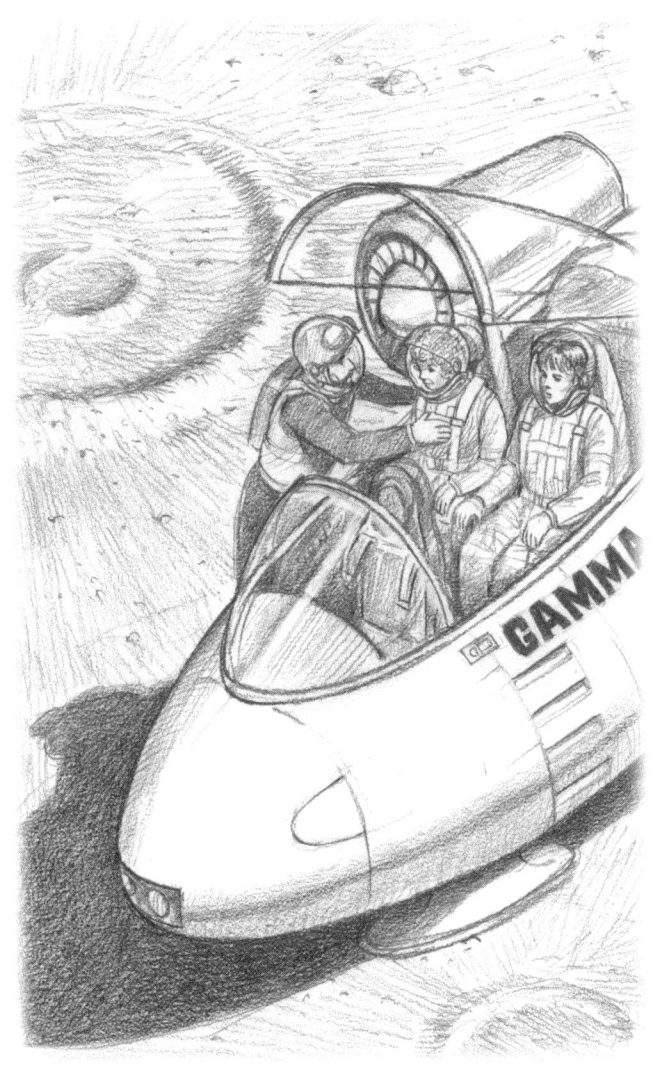

the need to be accurate. "Well, half a mile," he added.

Mr. Arjee smiled. "I believe you," he said.

"No, Dad, you don't," said Plata. "I can tell by your voice. But it's true. The caretaker came out of the ship, and he kept yelling at us to move away. My legs are just about broken."

"Plata!" Mr. Arjee turned to her. "I've had enough of this ghost talk. And there's no care-taker. There's never been a caretaker. No one is out here except us. Another thing, no one can get in or out of the old ship. It's sealed."

Plata had her hand over her wrist button to protest, but Conrad stopped her. He said to Mr. Arjee, "I'm sorry, sir. I think there's been some kind of mistake. The ship really does have a caretaker. He told us we had to go back because the waste in the ship was getting unstable. It was dangerous even outside the fence. He said you were going to do an air pollution test in a couple of days."

"I'm going to do *what*?" Mr. Arjee pulled down the jet cart cover with a snap.

"He said you would discover the high toxic levels around the ship. Then the waste will be taken away…"

"Conrad, that's enough!" Mr. Arjee sounded angry. "Of course I'm not doing any air pollution tests at the crash site. That's not part of my job." He slammed his hand down on the controls. "I leave you and Plata alone for twenty-five minutes and this is what you come up with."

Plata leaned forward. "Dad, he did say…"

"I said, enough, Plata!" Mr. Arjee lifted the jet cart off the surface and put it into thrust. He drove fast across the dust lake, creating a stormcloud of red dust behind them.

But Plata did not give up easily. In spite of a warning look from Conrad, she said, "His name is Jethro Anderson, and he's not imaginary!"

Mr. Arjee slowed the jet cart. "What did you say?"

"He's Jethro Anderson, and he's ..."

"Who told you that?" her father demanded.

"Mr. Anderson did," said Plata.

"No he didn't," said Mr. Arjee. "You got that from Conrad. Conrad heard his mother talking about Jethro Anderson."

"No sir," said Conrad. He was feeling very uncomfortable. He liked Mr. Arjee, and he didn't want to argue with him. "My mother has never mentioned Jethro Anderson. I'm sure she doesn't know him. You can ask her."

"I most definitely will ask her," Mr. Arjee said.

"Mom didn't even know there was a caretaker on the ship," said Conrad.

Mr. Arjee increased the thrust on the jet cart. "There is no caretaker," he said, but now he didn't sound angry, "and that can't be Jethro Anderson." He turned to them. "Jethro Anderson died more than two hundred years ago. He was commanding the shuttle when it crashed."

There was a moment of silence. Conrad and Plata stared at each other.

"Maybe," said Mr. Arjee, "I *will* do an air pollution test tomorrow."